"Immerse yourself in the enchanting spirit of the holiday season with our Country Christmas Coloring Book. This delightful coloring book transports you to a rustic winter wonderland, where charming scenes of cozy cottages, snow-covered landscapes, and festive farmsteads await your artistic touch.

Escape the hustle and bustle of modern life as you bring to life a collection of heartwarming illustrations that capture the essence of a country Christmas. Picture quaint barns adorned with twinkling lights, jolly snowmen standing guard in the fields, and horse-drawn sleighs gliding through the snow-covered countryside.

Each page is a canvas of creativity, inviting you to explore a palette of rich, festive colors. From the warm glow of fireplace interiors to the vibrant hues of traditional holiday decorations, let your imagination run wild as you infuse these charming illustrations with your own unique style.

Whether you're a seasoned coloring enthusiast or a newcomer looking for a relaxing holiday activity, our Country Christmas Coloring Book offers hours of joy and inspiration. Rekindle the magic of Christmas in a simpler time, where the beauty of the season is celebrated in every stroke of your coloring pencils or markers.

Gather around the virtual fireplace, sip on a cup of hot cocoa, and lose yourself in the nostalgic charm of a country Christmas. This coloring book is not just an artistic journey—it's a heartwarming escape into the timeless traditions and cozy comforts of a festive countryside celebration."

Merry Christmas!

from My Family To Yours

Please, Leave a review on Amazon
to help us out.

MERRY
CHRISTMAS

Home

Let it snow

LOVE

JOY

HAPPY

PEACE